Spirit Level

Mark Willing

Spirit Level

Spirit Level
ISBN 978 1 74027 704 4
Copyright © text Mark Willing 2011

First published 2011
Reprinted 2016

Ginninderra Press
PO Box 3461 Port Adelaide SA 5015
www.ginninderrapress.com.au

Contents

Steve	7
Debt Collection	8
Salt Plain	10
Perfect Wave	11
Potts Point '70	12
Burning Work	13
The Floating Pool	15
Secret Worlds	17
Dying Human	18
Enough	20
History of the Sock	22
Three Nights	24
Crossroads	25
The Right Angle	26
A Life of Colours	27
Adieu	28
Unattended	29
Times a Changing	31
nothing is more pure	33
Creation in First Person Singular	34
Structure	36
Late July	37
Cat's Skull	39
Dad Says Sad Days	41
Writing Rough	43
Blank Canvas Blues	44
The Lawn Cutters	45
'Arrogant with sky'*	46
Balcony	48
Spirit Level	50

Hitchhiking	52
White Water	53
fishing with robert	55
Shot-putter	56
Storm	58
Poem Meister	59
City/Sundown	61
Political Fishing	63
Thoughts on a Country Road	64
Converging Paths	65
The House and I	66
Satin Swallow	67
Smoking Balsa Wood	68
Leaf-Burning Saturdays	70
the candlelight poems	71

Steve

Sitting at the kitchen table
all night until sunrise
with a candle
and half a bottle of Scotch
writing the candlelight poems
not aware that you were watching
even understanding
why I do this
flashes of lightning
and rolls of thunder
through the open window
laughing my head off
at the ecstasy
of personal freedom
at the unshaven ballsy reflection
I could see in the tank's glass
raising my glass
my pen and a bicep
unaware of the eye
peering out at me
driving me home.

Debt Collection

Eight years old
our car reversing
out of the driveway
on our way
to collect debts
because that's our business
we remind people
they are fragile
that's our business.

As the car
is about to turn
into the street
a black shape swoops
from the tree
next to our driveway
an owl – says my father
and it rises up
into another tree
this time in our own yard.

The car idles
as we wait
for another sighting
but it just stays there
just outside the range
of our headlights.

Something must be lurking
in the garden below –
something with something
to repay.

The car rolls forward.
Come on – my father says –
we've got work to do.

Salt Plain

A little town
on the Eyre Peninsula
a girl called Miranda leaving
a fish and chip shop
cold sleety rain
on the bluestone promenade
with no one else walking
the gulls circling
the wind stinging
spray and sand from the shore
slicing the air
as she walks past
her wild brown eyes
for a split second embracing you
then looking away
into the loneliness
the terrible loneliness.

Perfect Wave

Since I was sixteen
the engine's been running
some would call it idle
but between
the serenities of inertia

came the high-rev dysfunctions
of a syncopated dancer

out of control
or hitch-hiking to Sydney

whenever/whatever
they ask me now
or later try to explain
somewhere between
a hymn and a pop song

will inevitably include
that splendid perfection
that bitter/sweet
most searched-for/never found
perfect wave

rolling us high and so far
in a wilderness of oceans
home.

Potts Point '70

That old fermentation sizzles
like lager wafting around the Point
                    classified crowds
stand outside nightclubs
chatting up bouncers

roy is walking hellbent
toward oxford street
talking about god and his daughter's
fantastic hot dogs

his legacy to his grandchildren
is his speed and invisibility
even at his age

roy and the dangerous night
locked up inside
pared into lines of sharp faces
not wanting to turn
to see what they'll become

blasphemous the nightingale's curse.

Burning Work

Burning work
in the old incinerator
an occasional leaf flaps about
in the hot aura
is beaten down to ash
with a long stake.

Is this how
it has to end?
        Always?
Let sleeping bodies lie.
The wind has a sniff
        of insomnia.
Smoke drifts across suburbs.
Funny how fire can be
so life-affirming.
When all is said and done.
When all is said.
Occasionally something is done.
The wet road mirrors an open sky.
Promise of sun glare
a flash pinpoint at the pinnacle.
Open sky mirrors an ocean
sucking light into its huge dark sun.
Embers fall into the sea.
There are no words remaining
in the gulf stream to explain
the science of currents
or the current science
of lifetime commitment

then a second's mad grace
the whiff the fume
the talking implosiveness
of art minus expression.
Fish and chips on the beach
watching the sun hovering down
rotor-bladed like brittle
pages to oblivion.

The Floating Pool

Juanita,
always the reckless one,
you had one chance to answer.
We are going out floating
in the pure white breath
of an Ampato sunrise
kicking the crystal flowers on the shore
of your terminal spring.

What were you thinking
what were they
when you hung upside down
and were called the 'empty-headed one'
by the elders and the tricksters.

Juanita,
I took you swimming.
Ripples barely left our sides.
I cradled your skull,
your motionless, matted hair
your dark Mongolian eyes,
I dragged you backwards
in a seated position
through a barricade of reeds –
statues and food scraps
locked in ice –
were not enough to make you smile.

I hear the villagers
talking in huddles.
It's still dark –
the cock yet to crow –
you've been sleeping in a bath
of your own fluids all night.
The blue of a far away sunrise,
the blue of your flesh, Juanita,
already in their mouths.

They took you out swimming
by the sides of the boats.
They left you, Juanita,
in the airless cavity
of your dark open mouth.
They thought they would be rid
of everything they could not explain.
They pointed you to the temple
of the sun, but instead,
Juanita, you froze.
Froze before all eternity.
Left to hang upside down
with no gold chain
around your smooth forehead.

Secret Worlds

My father played 'em on a break.
Who knows how many secret worlds
he carried around in his case
and how many I inherited?
His teeth were the first to go at a young age.
Then his large bowel
then small intestine
until finally, the liver, the kidneys
and the heart.
Gabrielle, the nurse, couldn't understand
how all the symptoms aligned by chance.
My father played 'em on a break.

Dying Human

I had had this fish
nine years and he was big
as half the tank was wide
and he wasn't much smaller
the day I got him
so I figured he must be
at least eighteen years old
most likely more

he died human
not like the smaller ones
who have come and gone
within the course of his memory
jack knifing or rolling around
the tank for weeks, even months
before being taken out
to end up in the infirmary bucket

he died with human suddenness
convulsing three times
then rolling on his side
onto a rock
we knew straight away
he was gone

for days after
all the smaller fish
filled the huge space
he had occupied above that rock
as if stretched to comprehend
what memory could not suffice
he was legend
their alpha and omega
in their revolving recollections

he died human
nothing understood
nothing and no one

we buried him in the yard
soil instead of cistern
a closure of sorts
his scales glowed
in his final moments of sunlight
his eye fixed on mine
as I pushed in the dirt
knowing, knowing
nothing and no one.

Enough

Always began
with the bravery
of too much wine
ended in a cross-country
through leafy streets
of a well-to-do school
sometimes the rapid
eye movement
during wet dreams
a piece of material
placed in the hand
at the scene of a murder
or names I'd never
heard before
being glued with vitriol
over all my body parts
a film in a back alley
about Kampuchea
so real a warlord
being led away
glanced over his shoulder
gave me a wink
eyes in the alley
doing that rapid movement
back in the head
during orgasm or death
or a villager
being bludgeoned
with his father's shoe
call it coincidence

call it the label
of the sum of moments

        so many things I don't understand!

like that day
on Young Adventurers Camp
when Chook got drunk
and did the Nerve Test
deciding enough was enough.

History of the Sock

Arthritis, the deeper meaning
of interpretive and critical
analysis, the underpinning
foot odour of the long journey
to enlightenment.
Salves and socks
flimsy pharmaceutical
ankle braces
all in the name of
witch doctory
or a Lazarus rising
in an out-of-sessions
tread and sole analysis.
Don't cut it
don't even penetrate
Herod's good council.
I believe Jesus went
most of the time
barefooted.
Knowing there were
others more adept
to God's earth
who knew every
bush and berry
its pain of existence
or lack of it
dosages handed down
by memory and mouth
in culture in deeper
rituals of the Rock

secret malarkeys
honey-tinged miracles
people walking upright
until told to drop.

Three Nights

Never understood
in the dark, the weird dark
around our edges, sleeping
in an outer room, I would
find you there beside me
when the magpie banter began.

For three nights we slept there
behind windows of wind and rain
your patchwork of fur pressed
to my old wounds, a cold front
advancing over your bony shoulder.
We both knew trouble in a wink.

Look down, at your feet,
sand.
Look up, stars.
Between us a taste
that has never been acquired.
But we travel still.

Crossroads

Coming to a crossroads
on the way to Sydney
discovering the complete
diversity of words
(if complete can be used in such context)
I set about sleeping in fields
somewhere to the side of Yass
a hilly paddock just out of sight
of the farmhouse and the highway
drizzling rain
        cows in the morning
                looking into
my sleeping bag
the white mist crossing the hills
like a traveller
        going before me
his songs, his silences
flowing in all directions
spreading with the speed
of wildflowers
before the season
encompasses them

The Right Angle

Time flies its temporary path.
Trajectories are infinite
as you sit and watch
all those things you once did
fly from my hands, my ignorant hands.
Your dark blue eyes trace threads
through the evening air.
You are putting up with the cold
our mock anguish
tickles your humour
makes you giggle a little
or pensively remember the pastimes
of caged bodies.
You are thinking to yourself
if the angle is right
you could close your eyes
and the sweet spot
would numb without trying.

A Life of Colours

Colours of background
>or of foreground
smokestack of hues
rising steadily above the rooftops
red in a bottle with mottled
sides, a canteen of laughter
with an amusement park of phobias
splaying around its weekend edges
violent meteors of primary ascents
and descents, never parallel, never
harmonic, blue of reposeful depths,
yellow idyll of ailing or healing
and the violet smudge of a waiting
room.
>Tympanic blacks
round out the motif of heart
beat in one last intimate drive
toward repose. Spectral array
and the hand of a nurse
slipping away.
>Then the silence.
Then the memories of background
>or of foreground.
Poems written in a pitch-black room.

Adieu

Needles keep me at bay
for most of the winter

occasionally we travel leeward
to the cosy garnet
of log fires with lounges

(didn't any of you see this coming?)

and before the voices waken for the day
we gather thoughts and time
for a few rousing verses
and the occasional quirky chorus

sometimes my head
crashes into
a mirror image of itself

silesh silesh I am alone now
no more drama to these hours
let the hand sleep
where it forms adieu.

Unattended

Showing me how to tend a camp fire.
You left no trace after.
Even beer bottles and cigarette butts.
Avoiding cafes.
We met philosophy halfway.
Showing me how to use a six iron.
For every position.
Any distance.
Eighteen holes of Kafka.
Tolstoy.
Marx.
Blowing my car horn at girls.
Commenting on my suburban frostiness.
Showing me how to pick red delicious.
Smoking to get rid of toothache.
Early morning Yarra orchard.
Freezing mist vomiting with cold.
A poem about Armstrong.
And you.
Years later in hell.
Picking you up to drive to that park.
Midnight midwinter.
Freezing out life's traumas.
Lighting a camp fire to keep warm.
Another poem – Moon Over Westerfolds.
Watching shadows writhe through the trees.
And not feeling afraid.
Your dog.
Your hand the back of it.
Every square inch.

The cry for help.
Sixteen years on.
The waiting.
The confession.
The burning corpse.
Down by the river by Neil Young.
The ash still smouldering.
Beneath the frost.
And all the inescapable secrets.

Times a Changing

Who would have believed it –
calcium dishing off stars
like radiation
in the milky way
calcium that may be harnessed
for a future super race of octogenarians
when I was young
they simply told us
you get calcium from milk
it's good for your bones
when I was young
I saw neil armstrong
walk on some rocks
on television
they say voyager
has been travelling thirty-three years
and can travel for millions more
and that lately it's been sending back
indecipherable messages
no computer can unravel
I once read a book
by james joyce
and I felt like my whole life
was being overtaken
by every chapter every page
the kobo e-reader allows users
to download and store up to
1,000 books displayed in easy-
on-the-eye digital ink
that looks and reads like real paper
it is being compared to the seismic impact

paperbacks had on the publishing industry
after world war 2
and figuratively the seismic impact
of radiation-charged particles
emitted from man-made devices
I'm reading about in a newspaper
in the driver's seat of a toyota
how humans are desperately
kneading the dough of god-like enterprise
forming synthetic cells
that will soon replace those
of the common cold or
even uncommon cancers
or even create whole beings
from the synthetic soup
of a synthetic ocean
so that when the bio-terrorists
get hold of it
to make mayhem or a super-race
we will all look back one day
from our synthetic eternal bubbles
and read about
the seismic impact
hayseeds had on humankind
since the third quartile
of the fifteenth holy jihad
when god-like creatures
attempted a human opera
in downtown neu yark province
on the site of old broadway
but failed the reviews.

nothing is more pure

than a single autumn leaf
lying in an arbour
of a pure white cathedral.

Creation in First Person Singular

After Gulley got started on his wall
I walked round the back
past the water tank on stilts
and made for the river
that was barely breathing. My stocks
low, my pages flicked with animate landscapes
rural by definition in the language
of urban history, I entered the rout
of creation and decency.
Forty years to the day,
Gulley found indecent proposals
in inner Sydney alleyways
as he turned his belief in humanity
into a galvanised ironic Eden
complete with mannequins, exotic apes,
fruit of deciduous temptation and original sin.
There was a blonde woman
screaming get the hell off my property
in a Eurovision Song Contest
kind of diaphragmatic bludgeoning.
There was a man on the ground
and another kicking him
to see if he was still alive,
a third joined in because he was a graduate
of Gulley's 'the fall' that was transported from Manchester
around the Cape of Good Hope
and into Fremantle where it was propped like a sculpture
overlooking 'small portions of the eternal world'.

Meanwhile, the national gallery beckoned
and Gulley went in search of its huge north facing wall
looking like a flicked page of an animate landscape
with rural fingers digging for history,
the concierge with puffed-up political correctness
directing a line of perfect limousines
which, to Gulley, a parliament of owls would have proffered
something more modern, their jutting ridge just below a setting sun
and a crag of crows snuffing the last vestiges
of Eden in a drought-resistant new order.

Structure

I'm thinking of a structure

a bit like the blocks
in Man Ray poetry

always with you
even without words

a structure of future tense
highly seductive

drawing language out of you
with holiness and perfect fit

I was sixteen
when the structure first appeared

as solids of *Te Deum*
the blocks jumped out

and down the page
the ringing chords

created and shaped them
I was left standing in only future tense.

Late July

(for Rob)

Night of whispered surmise;
the cold winds have arrived
and I sit outside on the veranda,
your wine a lifetime maturing.

We sat this way
on an evening late July
one more year ago
than the years since you died,

the cigars tasting fresh,
that smell of oak sharpness,
our lateral conversation
loosening with each port.

You never drank
so I took it as an honour
as much as the chance
to be a part of your life.

What do males have
in the distances and the silences,
larrikin ideals?
superman tendencies?

I can remember
looking away to the skyline,
the city, the buildings
and being warmed by their closeness.

Like so many suburbs
we had occupied over the years,
it seemed we had shared
more houses than words.

So now I sit and wonder
if it was true what we surmised
and if you had time to leave a sign.

I look at the stars and I wonder.

Cat's Skull

The skull was buried
in the backyard
twelve inches below the topsoil.
I carried it in a clear plastic bag
for effect.

The class marvelled at the hairline crack
running from the nose to the nape.
The skull travelled with me
for years after
trying to wrench life from death
trying to distinguish bone from ideal.

Mutant discoveries were never enough.
The bone was only the misunderstood
that surrounded a cortex of mystique.

What we have received
discoveries calcified
are calculations of the unrequited.

What we have done
stares back from emptiness
as multiple guilts

yet the soft wet-earth memory
adheres to the skull

a falling to earth
landing in soft hands
and the jagged ructions
of shape and image:

Reprise the one constant after life
and love – a silent, invisible act.

The importance of showing
what I couldn't understand
left speechless with the ringing of the bell.

Dad Says Sad Days

Dad says sad days
are dearer than a pint of ale
and willow on leather can't be that inflated

dad says sad days
are overrun by peace movements
and the more secret SAS wanting
terrorists to secretly win

dad says sad days
are a bride taken
before the twenty-fifth date
or a divorce taken
before the twenty-fifth year

dad says sad days
are warmer than past years
but only in some parts
where they've heard of greening
and global warming

dad says sad days
are a lost picnic under the elms
at the Fitzroy gardens
where families saunter in shock
admiring global financial crisis lilies
not floating in the drought-dry lake

dad says sad days
are poetically tragic
but publicity balanced
by rapid-eye technology
promoted under the premise
of certain social groups
actually getting off their arses
and being positively resourceful

dad says sad days
come at you
like a high country sunrise
full of orange
and man from snowy river
red guts
blowing in little red embers
through the arid spinifex
everywhere

because we've changed
as a nation
and in our hearts
and we'll never go back
dad says.

Writing Rough

Like the Valkyries of ancient poetry
after rites of holy kinship have been explored
preparing to ride toward Valhalla
there are points of access and touch
which cannot be explained by tribal law.
Journeys continue by feel.
Wonders, not triumph, access motion and time.
They wait until all guests are gone.
Conversations divert from theory to silence.
Fluent meditation, economy of meaning
take place in the single utterance of distance.
Parlour music takes on the dimming of light.
Things must be written, whether worded or wordless.
Like the compression of desire
left to touch and recreate
upon the contour of the ethereal breast.
Whisky and candlelight
and that old stricture of chest pain
should be smothered with no feminine lamentation
and with no tears, save the blood of men
diverting reality into fears of
not what will be missed in death
but what will fail to be achieved in life.

Blank Canvas Blues

I watch and listen to people
who blindly shut the door
behind spider webs. Old arcades
intrigue with their tunnel secrets
dark air and candle-warm interiors

everyone walks around in circles
with blank canvases under their arms
they look busy, make themselves look busy
rolling out futures as near-red carpets
pulling the rug from their dusty pasts

rooms with secret panels seduce
with the smell of murder and
cape fear thrill. Glasses poured with
three-quarter adrenalin age patiently
upon the scratched sideboard

visible fumes rise from a blanket
like cigar smoke, maybe a spirit
and the blank canvas pulses
with fluorescent idiosyncrasies
webbed and tangled with the passing of years
and brilliant ideas.

The Lawn Cutters

Mid-morning, the lawn cutters
come with grass high regularity,
strolling along behind
their high rev conversations,
talking to themselves, creating
music they will sleep with
comfortably at night.
Theirs is the low, vibrant
hum of fitless dreams
and they arrive at the first
sign of onion weed with
laughter in their tawny voices.

Later that night,
unable to sleep,
I wonder at their music
and their laughter, and I think
my life must be missing something:
that low humming perseverance,
or the monotonous tick of a clock on the wall,
or even somebody's voice alongside me –
something, anything
to break the overgrown silence.

'Arrogant with sky'*

Late November
leaving the Mercy
in East Melbourne

something made us
look skyward –
something we were yet to know –

a group of thirty or so
fawn and black bats
heading into the CBD.

For the next fortnight
a sole bat
came to live
in the fruit trees
of our property.

Each night
with a giant wingspan
pumping some
hydra pressure within

it would rise
into the dark,
circle two or three times,
then glide like a harrier
onto its moonlit deck.

I knew
in those
great swishing wing beats

it was telling me
how flight
is not the sky it has missed,
but the world it has firmly left behind.

*(from The Flashing Mountain by Dorothy Porter)

Balcony

The balcony looked over
Parliament Place

one of those you escape to
through a body length
window

I used to sit
one storey up
watching the moratoriums
marching by

reading the placards
watching the young girls
in tight summer clothes
holding hands with revolutionary boyfriends

it was spring '70
but it could have been Czechoslovakia '68
the time was right
for balmy anarchy

after they had all gone
home to the suburbs
I'd walk down at midnight
to the Treasury Gardens
with a bottle of beer

sit on a bench
and wait for that other parade
slowly sauntering by
the real revolutionaries

living in a paradise
of uncombed hair
no money
and a canopy of trees

the world they wanted to change
had already changed

Spirit Level

As a family, sucked into a whirlpool
of cliché, metaphor or stereotype
always the last to desert a game of beach cricket
because of poor light or water-drawn lightning
sketches found in a gladstone bag
closely resembling sophia loren
a pouting countenance, foraged bank accounts
awol for months, a stint in solitary
we were always solitary whether at home or at church
and Sunday was often a day of venting
always a chip off the old block
we were sopranos, pianists, writers, money launderers,
water diviners, hooch sellers, sunday school superintendents
balance was most revered in a cover drive
not as that rare grace at the spirit level
the kind that leads others from the darkness
or reconciles scars of wounded integrity
we were rudderless in that divined inland sea
and we seemed to have arrived from the four corners
stateless refugees, or a colonial mismatch
of aryan-cockney and to the four corners
we dispersed, educated or plain bullish
and being the youngest, I was always the child
happy to live there, always will be
in a fertile, escapist magician's act
called imagination, art or close-to-the-bone faith
never knowing if it was scar tissue or redemption
never rocked the boat
always the one to keep it steady
like a flatline hypnotic command of waves

coming up from behind, larger than houses
standing up to my waist
waiting for that cover drive
that would never come in this darkness
and the lightning rendering the spaces to oblivion.

Hitchhiking

Dropping in on Sydney
– some called it living –
in 1970 was calligraphy
without a mother tongue

our skin was so tight
we could barely walk
bartenders tended not to believe it
but some of the hookers
wanted us to be over eighteen.

I remember my first shot of the bridge
– writing my one and only play in Hyde Park –
a still, grey, world-wonder
metallic arches beckoning through skyscrapers
waiting to take me
north of everything I had ever known.

White Water

Sometimes I wake up
from a dream of
a wall of white water
coming straight at me.

My father and I
would go fishing
on the bay
in a trawler
of up to twenty men.

They'd always move
to the other side
of the boat
joking that we
were bad luck.

One day
my father hired
a metal dinghy.
As we cruised out
across the calm river
towards open water
a wall of turbulence
was waiting up ahead.

My father turned
the dinghy around.
'Can't go out today son.'
I cried the whole way
back to the jetty.
My father said
we'd been given a sign.

Years later
a week before he died
he lay in his hospital bed
and said
'sorry.'

His eyes chiselled
into mine
with the look
he had that day
in the dinghy –
that day of
the wall of white water.

fishing with robert

hawkesbury midnight in a half moon
we flick another lure
out into impossible darkness
something like firefly flashes past
we glance at each other, smiling
– there goes another one –
our drunken skiff rolls uncontrollably
then once again only the plop of optimism
alluring to the forest, the sky, the world
in all of this form, intellect, multi-edition
livre-libre
for every one a million others
slipped through the nets of a million more.

Shot-putter

He mowed a little strip
of grass behind the chook shed
where they used to park the plough
in the off season. Days were full
then; life a constant rippling of muscle
and a bale took in a good dollar.
He cut it to a height
where the silver spheres
stood out waiting to be picked up
and to be put back again.
Day after day he applied the physics
of Newtonian arrogance,
(hope that goes up must come down,
but defend your petulance
long enough for maximum distance.)
He learned to embrace the smooth curve
in the warm arch of his neck.
He applied his own barn dance memory
to the hop-stepping approach.
He finally got an invitation
to the institute of sport.
Fitted out and shipped off
to another country
he stood in the stadium
in a strange kind of euphoria
where crowds of the ordinary kind
are not allowed to enter.
The big Games' hope,
the wonder from the bush,

the dark horse farm boy
tossing it in with the best.
He came somewhere in the middle of the field.
He might have been on for a medal
if, in the approach to his final attempt,
the thought of his father,
the chook shed and the broken-down plough
hadn't crossed his mind.
Like the realisation
that life is very ordinary
even at the highest moments
because it is firmly embedded
in the rules of its normality,
the normality of its rules.

Storm

Tender papal kissing of hands
or the magpie's drop-dead gorgeous song
in the crisp, fermented fume of daybreak
the entry of words I do not know
let fall at the feet of the other
in their isolation or juxtaposition
like a storm smashing into chrysalis shells
no two raindrops behave the same
but the laws of spectra burning in these hands.

Poem Meister

This city encapsulates
moods
of the seventies
with a bottle of blue nun
tucked
under the heart
a moratorium
to attend
or a church service
for the last piece
of your faith
like the first time
you tried beer
you were suddenly
free
to make your own
blurry decisions
and the women
in all dimensions
were enough
to start
a nuclear war
this was the seventies
we were children
in adult costumes
the proliferation
of art nouveau
was coming
to an end
but in strange ways
from balconies

we were yet to rent
was about to
breed
words of
indiscriminate
direction
the war continued
and optimism graced
the more silent members
of the study group
who over time
got drafted
or died
in drunken car
accidents
the one preacher
of my soul
had escaped
the fire
and had gone
to live in paradise
with an American passport
and a false name
that rhymed with
bob. The times
were certainly a changing
bells of freedom rang
and telephones were
being fitted out
with triple O
fast tracks.

City/Sundown

Huge blocks of shadow
rectangular nightshade
with little pimples of office
light
yellow and scarlet
reflections
off the yarra
running parallel
with the night train
of oscar peterson
and an old record
over which
a wavery needle
scratches the skin
vinyl blurs
inside the head
of a porter outside
the southern cross

this city guides us
away over fields
to the audience
who keep coming back
to its heart/its spirit
akhmatova and jazz
and forgotten readings
in and around
the inner laneways and hotels
as if sparking
inside a kerosene tin

flint traffic
in the ancient night

the alluring
musical night

Political Fishing

Lucidity is a form of recompense
for those times when the mind is clouded over
when people look at you as if every failure
was your own fault; an escape from the confusion
it has its place in prayer, meditation and surrender
it has its place at the heart of the strivings of creativity
art is surrender
to all anarchies and confusions, to chaos and lawlessness
and above all
failure
art kicks on long after the party
lucidity flows like vaccine through cells
we are ecstatic and pained to entertain
the lucid moment worth ten thousand lifetimes
it spawns ransoms, poetry, constitutions and song.

Thoughts on a Country Road

I never dream;
I only wake up after dreaming.

I never had a mother tongue;
I only wrote words which arrived as poems.

A nation without poets
is a mother who never raised a child.

There is no evidence of a soul;
but that girl on the promenade looked straight through me.

God is a wayfarer;
all roads lead to the blind spot in your mirror.

Converging Paths

A black bat
is cruising around
our eastern sky

the rain leaves
a dark pall
across the mountains

my cat's eye
purrs in a separate
knowledge

across vast miles
of memory
all things are
faintly joined

we have our reason
solutions are never reached.

The House and I

A little less crowded now
we suck heat through infra-red straws
we search for bumps behind the curtains
case the letter box before we enter

more room for intruders
means less for comfort
this house has changed

its irons squeak softly
its timbers pull apart
there's brushing outside the bedroom window
azaleas whisper in pale blue streetlight

more alone than ever
the house and I sleep
with our heat divided

and tracing inarticulate dawn
we stroke each other's surfaces
wiping clean all evidence
of us.

Satin Swallow

A satin swallow

flashes
off the trees
of an evening sky

its feathers
smoother
than air

elevate
my eyes
to the first
star of night

then dart
into permutations
of free fall
obtuse diagonals

and i pray
if this is the path
of a God i cannot
track

then so be it.

Smoking Balsa Wood

Neat strips
sliced with a
tenet saw

matches stolen
from the bottom drawer

down the back
crouched between ferns
when everyone was at work.

It was extremely
sexual.
Chook
said he could
get a hard-on
after two puffs.

The porous
element
of pre-adolescent
desire

let through
sifted
like playboy pages
worth tearing.
The smoke
inhaled
then streamed out
like fathers did

the smell
of scorched wood
imitating Craven A

in the backwoods
of telepathic
Freudian mystery

in the excuses
being planned
before the plan
went up in smoke.

Leaf-Burning Saturdays

Feet dangling over the edge of the prow
squealing at possible shark sightings
my father wheelbarrowing me out to sea
and the current soft landing of the leaf pile
I would watch as he shovelled them into the drum
and sparking a match at the invisible root
set light to sunrise and sunset as one
light plumes of smoke and gasoline
delighted in blurring the boundaries of suburbs
gaining heaviness over roofs and clothes lines
greying before settling their ash and their odours
my father incinerating paper shopping bags
filled with debts, receipts and brochures
the clouds swirled higher into the city
the hills and beyond into god knows where
their leaf-smoke harbouring some deeper belief
his eyes transfixed as if at a cremation
leaf-burning tunes whistling from his lips
as I searched upward for that familiar void
of column around column where smoke would disappear
rearrange then reappear in another sky as if
one world, swallowed by another, would emerge
from the horizon, as if whole revelations of white
would slide past others and in the space between
immerse in my father's biblical shroud
until he would gradually sharpen through the thinning haze
his laugh almost evil, his hands raised upward
and the garbage of his world, his debtors forgiven
slowly eradicated from the natural order.

the candlelight poems

1

humid night
a fly
a candle

the storm
came from the west
knocked down some power lines

in semi-darkness
i re-evaluate my life
epiphanies come and go
this house is growing
away from me

soon there will be
nothing left
but dark air

i set my sights
on a new
revolution

rain squeezes
in solitary drops

everything struggles

and the oppressive air
has that sense
of foreboding

the fly goes close
to the flame

i pour a drink
midnight passes
chainsaws in the distance

happy australia day!

2

i don't want you
to screw up
with festival bulbs

i don't want
your electric skin
to shine

give me raw
candle power
with the capacity
for love
at twenty paces

as my shadows move
into concentric body parts

let me
eat
all that is forbidden

let me
eat
flame.

3

i always
used to think
there was the perfect poem

and that is what drove me
to write

now i sit translucent
before the spitting flame

people still snigger
but i've just changed the name
like collector to writer

but in my mind
it's all still the same

i have the key
they have no idea.

4

don't tarnish with pages
what you can do
yourselves, my people

the roach prays diligently
upon my table
of fruit and absinthe

when i blow
he freezes
the candle extinguishes

and he and i
are left alone in darkness –
a blank page

for fantastic obsession.

5

being a jester
of surprising surmise

handclapping adoration
for the naked flame

the tearaway lyricist
rhymes something with orange

out of a revered
storm sunset

and his name
sky-written

on all walls of the forum
we call aurora.

6

listening to rain
in candlelight

falling on the roof

ocean waves
to a blind man

a symphony
of invisible forces

intangible cantatas

this is my life
this is my home

this is
all i was bred for

7

a bottle of highland legend
some tchaikovsky on the turntable
(6th symphony i think)
a packet of p j ones
and some corn chips

a candle burning
in a vegemite glass
and some books
as ancient
as hieroglyphics

turn life around

keep the world revolving

at exactly thirty-three and a third.

www.ingramcontent.com/pod-product-compliance
Lightning Source LLC
LaVergne TN
LVHW011739060526
838200LV00051B/3241